GOOD VIBES ONLY

Journal

Written by Susie Rae
Illustrated by Lizzy Doyle

ARCTURUS

ARCTURUS

This edition published in 2022 by Arcturus Publishing Limited
26/27 Bickels Yard, 151–153 Bermondsey Street,
London SE1 3HA

Author and Editor: Susie Rae
Illustrator: Lizzy Doyle
Designer: Rosie Bellwood
Editorial manager: Joe Harris

ISBN: 978-1-83940-822-9
CH008267NT
Supplier 29, Date 0522, Print run 11341

Printed in China

This book
belongs to:

Carsyn
Ann
Rausch

You Do You!

Whether you're a dreamer or a planner, a writer or an artist, a thrillseeker or a chill-seeker, this journal is the perfect place for you to be yourself. This is a space where you can plan your madcap schemes, flex your creative muscles ... or just make a massive, satisfying mess! It's totally up to you.

Go on a sunrise/sunset walk on the beach

This is top of my travel to-do list

I want to go here!

Flordia or Hawaii

MY TUNES

Hey best friend, I made a playlist of songs I think you'd love!

Cruel summer

These songs need to be played **AS LOUD AS POSSIBLE**

THIS SONG IS THE BEST

Happy Memories

These memories make me
smile every time **I** think
about them.

Fashion Goals

Take a look at this new look I'm creating—
everything about it just screams ME.

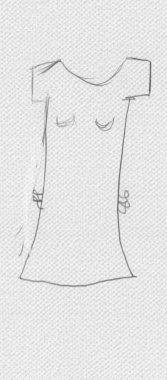

Blue

Family Tree

There's no place like home! Here are some of the people (and animals) I call family ...

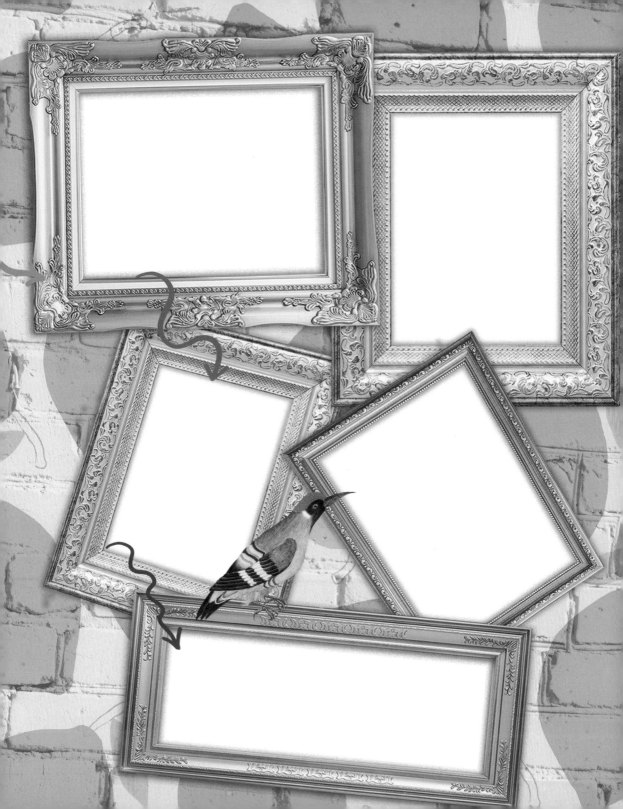

Haikus

Haikus are mini poems with three lines, like this:

5 SYLLABLES

7 SYLLABLES

5 SYLLABLES

Haikus are easy.
Five beats, then seven, then five.
Now you have a go!

It's amazing what you can say in so few words!

GET CREATIVE

Let's create something brand new from these weird shapes.

Life's so much more FUN when there's no wrong answer.

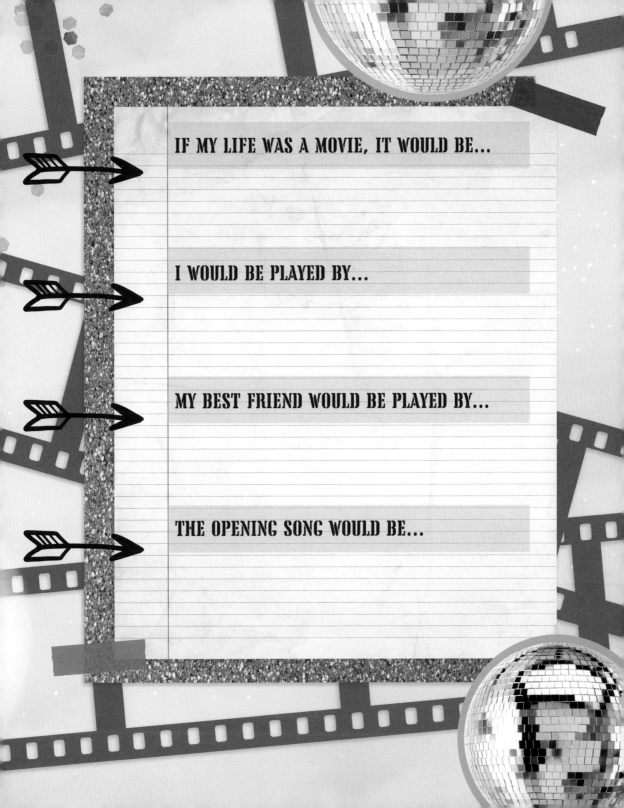

IF MY LIFE WAS A MOVIE, IT WOULD BE...

I WOULD BE PLAYED BY...

MY BEST FRIEND WOULD BE PLAYED BY...

THE OPENING SONG WOULD BE...

WILD AT HEART

Some people believe that we were different animals in our past lives. If that's true, then I'm pretty sure I would look like this ...

Let it Grow

Here's an amazing plant I grew (or found).
This is what it looked like when it started out.

Here it is after two weeks ...

... and a month.

Field notes:

Eventually, I hope it'll
look like this!

Page Turner

You're not supposed to judge a book by its cover ...

but this cover I designed for a book I love is pretty cute.

MAKE YOUR MARK

It's time to grab as many different paints, inks, and weirdly shaped objects as I can find. I'm going to make a work of art!

Meet Your Heroes

When I get the chance to meet my
idol, these are all the things
I'm going to ask them.

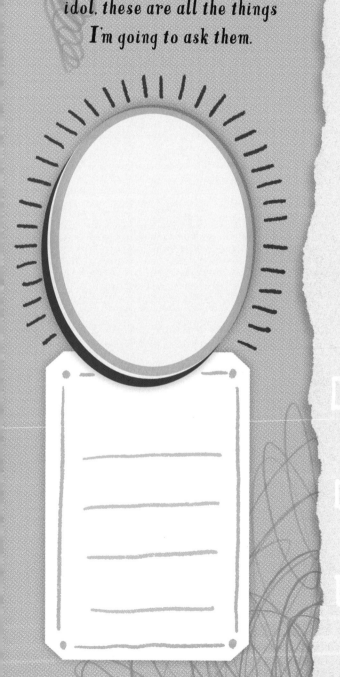

I've had this for years.

Me, Myself, and I

If you want to get to know me, these six objects can tell you so much about who I am.

THROWBACK

This is what I looked like when I was younger. I'm so different now!

Look how cute I was!

Some of the ways
I've changed:

Recipe for Success

I'm going to find out how to make all the different
food that I love. Here are some amazing recipes.

Written in the Stars

What's written in the stars?
This is what I see when I look up.

This is what I can see from my bedroom.

BEST PLACE EVER

Of all the places in the world, this is the one I love the most.

HISTORIC
— 25 - 9 —
1975
POLAND

NEW ZEALAND
11 SEP 1992

There's so much
to see!

Rule the World

If I was in charge, I could make the world a way better place. Here are my plans for (super chill) world domination ...

Make Your Wave

ON MY BOOKSHELF...

This book makes me laugh.

I've read this book so many times.

Dear Future Me...

I'M CURRENTLY ... YEARS OLD.

THE MOST IMPORTANT THINGS IN MY LIFE ARE ...

MY BEST FRIEND IS ...

IN THE FUTURE, I
HOPE I'M DOING ...

I'D LOVE TO LIVE HERE:

THE MOST IMPORTANT THING YOU SHOULD REMEMBER IS ...

INTERIOR DESIGNER

Here are some stylish improvements that I'd love to make to my bedroom.

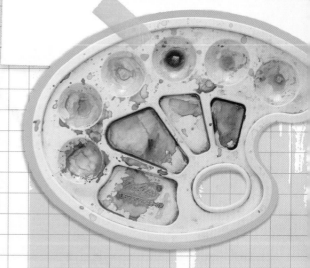

Trying out different paints and patterns

Getting the vibe right

Style inspiration

Best Friends

Saving the World

I'M GOING GREEN! HERE ARE SOME WAYS I CAN HELP THE PLANET

The future's bright!

Making these tiny changes can make a huge difference

Silver Linings

This is what **I** see when **I** look up at the clouds.

The sky is always changing.

Stars in Your Eyes

People used to think that the stars told stories—and I totally see why! Here are the stories I think the stars are telling.

I'm writing a song! These are some early ideas ...

SONGWRITER

My music inspirations

Reel Life

I COULD WATCH THESE TV SHOWS AND
MOVIES <u>ALL DAY.</u>

Inspiring
Artists

This artist really speaks to me.

I wish I could make art like this.

Plant Life

Who doesn't love nature? This piece of art is inspired by the great outdoors.

I love flowers!

Lost & Found

I'm going to find ...

two things that rhyme ...

something red ...

something
round ...

something sweet ...

Oh look!

I thought I'd
lost that.

Collector

Everybody has something that they love to collect! Here's mine.

I love this one the most.

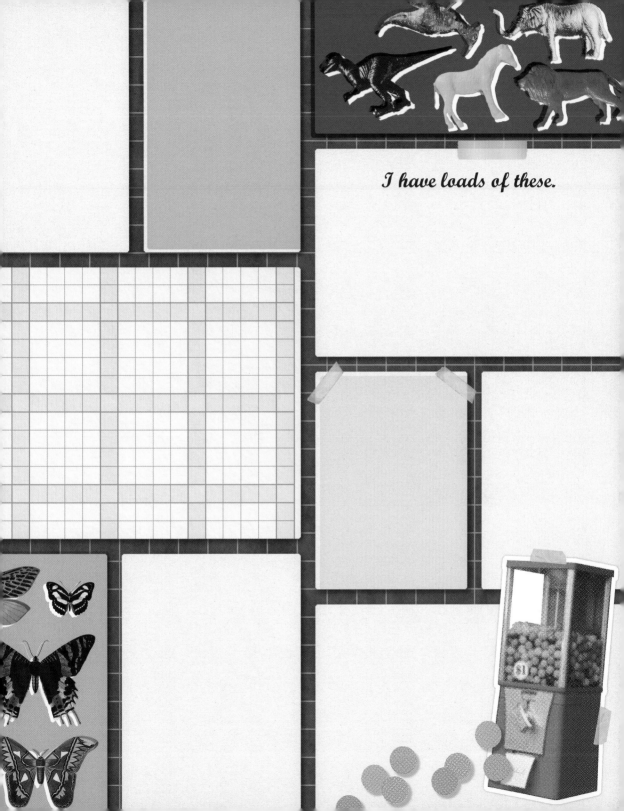

I have loads of these.

On the Menu

Come over for dinner! Here's what I'll be cooking.

Work of Art

I'm creating a piece of art using different shapes
and shades. What do you think?

Listen Up

There's so much to notice when you take a minute to slow down. Here are all the things I can hear around me when I close my eyes and take a deep breath.

The world is amazing when you take the time to notice things!

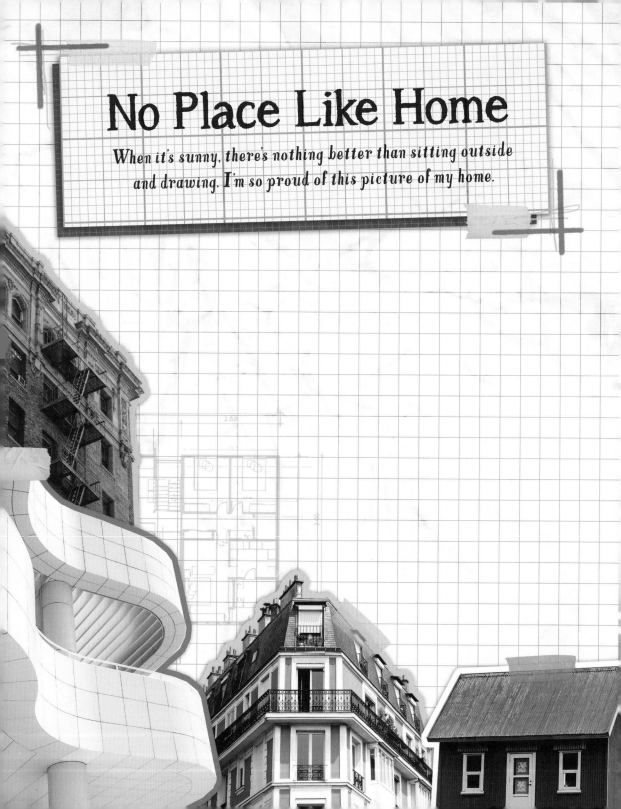

No Place Like Home

When it's sunny, there's nothing better than sitting outside and drawing. I'm so proud of this picture of my home.

Role Models

These people inspire me so much.

Story Prompts

It was a dark and stormy night ...

Some things have to be seen to be believed ...

These three words changed my life ...

A long time ago, in a distant land ...

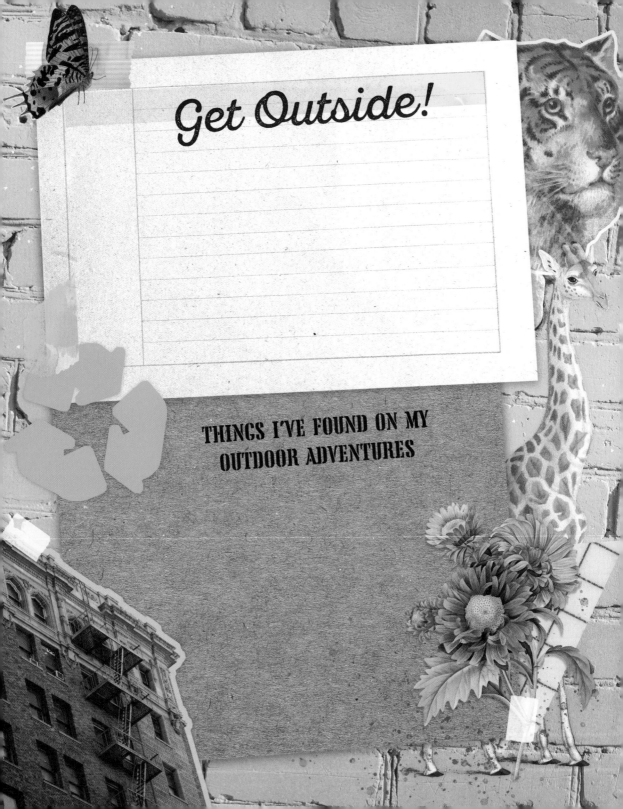

Get Outside!

THINGS I'VE FOUND ON MY OUTDOOR ADVENTURES

I never expected to find this!

I'm really good at this.

My
Dream Job

Plans for how to get there

This would be
really fun.

Local Wildlife Explorer

You don't need to go on safari to see some incredible creatures! Look what I've found outside my own front door.

Don't scare them away.

Hello, friend!

Outfit Collage

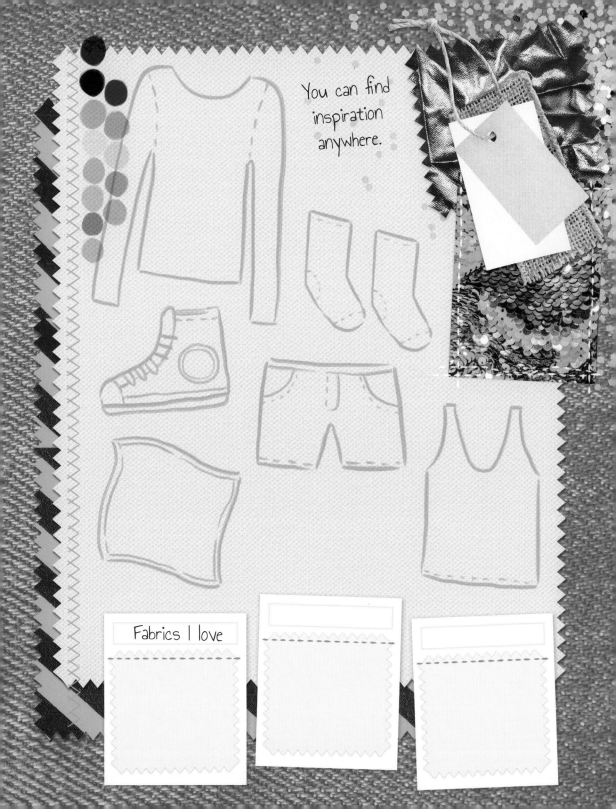

You can find inspiration anywhere.

Fabrics I love

CHAOTIC ENERGY

Sometimes I feel utterly anarchic. I'm going to fill this space with complete chaos! Scribbling, random words ... there's no limit!

(IT'S MY BOOK, SO IF I WANT TO TEAR THIS PAGE OUT, WHY SHOULDN'T I?)